DO

BETTER

THINGS

The 4 Traits of
Innovative Leaders

John Storta Jr

ISBN: 979-8-9852138-0-5

First paperback edition November 2021

Shenanigans Media
PO Box 1963
Concord, NC 28026

johnstortajr.com
shenanigansmedia.com

For my parents
You believed in me

CONTENTS

INTRODUCTION

LED bulbs are ubiquitous today. They are bright, efficient, cheap, and it is hard to imagine how we could improve on them. Yet, before we had LEDs, we used compact fluorescents (CFLs). Before the CFLs, there was Edison's incandescent. Before that, it was gas lamps and candles and oil lamps. Each of these inventions was a revolution in lighting. Each was the pinnacle of technology. Yet, somehow, each was later supplanted by something new. Even today's LED will eventually give way to something better.

Innovation requires that we never become content with where we are. We must believe that an even better solution is out there for the taking. Rather than make a better incandescent bulb, what if we designed an entirely new way to create the light? Don't just try to do things better. Strive to do better things.

But how does one do that?

The key is to not get hung up on the destination. Innovation is rarely about a miracle discovery that happens overnight. Innovation is a long process built upon failed attempts and missteps.

Indeed, despite pop culture attributions to the contrary, Thomas Edison did not even invent the incandescent bulb. He bought the patent from a pair of Canadians that were unable to market it. Their invention was built on the work done by a dozen others over the preceding century. The incandescent light bulb was not an 'a-ha' moment in a lab. It was the final chapter of a long story.

Too often, we look at success only from the perspective of that last chapter. Lindberg flying the Atlantic. Neil Armstrong walking on the moon. The Berlin Wall coming down. These events did not happen on a whim. They were the culmination of years of dedicated work that ultimately paid off.

The people that made these things happen were no different than you or me. What allowed them to succeed was their commitment to innovation. They were willing to take risks. They did not get bogged down in how things are. They focused on how things might be. When they encountered problems, they persevered and found a way forward. Being an innovative leader is about developing the tools needed to blaze a new trail and not being afraid to use those tools.

Let's consider the moon landings. Hindsight allows us to trace the path backwards from Neil Armstrong's walk in 1969 all the way to Kennedy's address to congress in 1961. When viewed from this direction it looks like this group had all the answers from the very beginning. This is only because all the failed plans they tried along the way have been filed away in the archives of history. All we see now is the clear roadmap to success.

But their success was not the result of foresight into how to accomplish the goal. They were certainly smart, but they did not know the path when they started. Their accomplishment was due to their innovative spirit and determination at each step along the way. Their ability to write the first hundred chapters is what allowed them to be successful in the last one.

A few years ago, I was doing research into media companies and came across this quote in the Netflix employee onboarding guide.

If you want to build a ship, don't drum up people to collect wood and don't assign them tasks and work, but rather teach them to long for the endless immensity of the sea.

—Antoine de Saint-Exupéry—

This quote captures the essence of what innovative leadership should be. Leaders don't tell people what to do. They inspire others to reach beyond where they are and strive for something greater. The leader doesn't have the roadmap. The leader knows how to inspire others to create it. If the leader does their job well, they can unite an entire team toward a common purpose. It is that shared purpose that brought down the Berlin wall. It is that innovative spirit that allowed humans to walk on the moon.

All great discoveries from history began with a vision—an idea that something better could be achieved. Those visions were shared with others who were inspired to join the cause. Along the way, open lines of communication ensured the best possible decisions were being made. And, every person involved recognized that continuing education is the only way to sustain growth for the long haul.

Vision. Inspiration. Communication. Education. These traits are at the core of all innovative leaders. In this book we will go through everything you need to unlock these traits within yourself so that you can strive to do better things.

WHAT KIND OF LEADER
WILL YOU BE?

Leaders take many forms. Some observe and calculate, always considering the next move on the board. Others are more direct, speaking their mind and sorting out the details later. Some are completely in tune with their team on a personal level, while others focus on the business goals alone. These different leaders can be right, and they can be wrong.

The first time you take on a position of leadership, you will face many new challenges. This is the beginning of the journey. Your team does not know you. They are unsure what kind of leader you are. They do not know what is expected of them or what their role truly is. They have a passing idea of where they are going but have more questions than answers. They look to you for those answers, but before you can have any chance of doing so, you must ask yourself, "What kind of leader will I be?"

If you take too much control, no one will learn to do tasks themselves. If you step too far back, the team may struggle with direction. If you get too close to your team, they might not respect you as a leader. If you are too distant, they may feel you do not care about them. It is a balancing act that is unique to each team.

As you develop in your leadership career you will no doubt complete many classes and read many articles that walk you through what to say in different circumstances. In many cases, these materials will have scripts you can follow for different conversations and even responses. They may even provide a checklist of steps for every scenario. But no checklist should be followed blindly. The creator of those materials can only speak at a general level. They have no way of knowing the situation you are in or the personalities of the people on your team. Even this book is a guide that can only offer tips from someone who has walked the path. I cannot speak to every scenario you will encounter.

Imagine yourself an airline pilot. You go

through a ton of training and spend numerous hours in the simulator. There are checklists for various events that could transpire, but no two events are alike. All the checklists can provide you with is the guide for the recommended best practices. There is no guarantee that those practices will apply to your situation.

On January 15, 2009, US Airways flight 1549 took off from LaGuardia airport in New York City. At an altitude of just 2,800 feet, the plane struck a flock of Canadian geese and lost power from both engines. The flight crew had checklists on how to deal with a loss of power and how to restart engines and many other conditions they were now facing. But none of those checklists covered what to do if you are only 2,800 feet above the ground and flying over the fourth largest metropolitan area in the world. All the training and all the checklists can only get you so far.

Being a leader means you must be able to apply that knowledge to any number of situations and make the best decisions. Those decisions will be partly based on experience, partly on training, and partly based on your personal code. Where those circles overlap is where you will be driven. If you have not defined who you are, then you will flounder.

You will struggle to make a choice when the training and the experience are not aligned.

In the case of US Airways flight 1549, the training said to try to get back to the airport. Captain Sully's experience told him he would never make it. He needed a third input to tip the scales or else he would become frozen in the decision-making process. That third input was himself. He was aware of his capabilities and the situation and what the plane could do. This awareness, which cannot be put in a checklist, is what allowed him to act.

So, who are you?

Think of the leaders you have encountered thus far in your career. Which ones were the most helpful to you? Which ones made you strive to be better? Who gave you the confidence to advance? Who made you a better person? These are the leaders you are striving to be.

Now get more specific. Ask yourself what they did that you found most valuable. If you valued those things, then they are worth something to you and likely others. Make a list of those things and choose the top three. You cannot possibly try to be everything. Choose the three things that you most want to be. You can certainly keep the other things handy, but make sure you have three that will be your guideposts for who you are.

And do not overlook the other side of this coin. Think of leaders that you hated. What did they do that didn't sit well with you? Did they demean you personally? Did any of them get upset at the slightest infractions? Were you reprimanded when you didn't do things the way they would have done it? Were you motivated only by a fear of failure? Make sure you highlight those behaviors as things you want to avoid.

As you go through this exercise, I want you to specifically think back to your earliest jobs. Everyone's career is different, but generally we all started in some hourly role doing a task that is easy to teach someone and pays little. Think all the way back to those jobs.

These experiences are great opportunities to assess leaders. In these roles, you are the lowest of the low in the food chain. You are easily replaced and are providing minimal value. In essence, you are a necessary evil for the business.

Meanwhile, your leaders at these jobs are generally people who are doing this as a career. They are professional supervisors or managers. They have a stake in the operation. The question is, how do they treat you? You can accurately assess who a person is by how they treat those that have nothing to offer them. All you have to offer is your ability to open a box, or lift something, or dial a phone, or a dozen other easily teachable tasks. Important work for the company, but a chore that usually requires little training and has a long waiting list of people that can do it if you do not work out. You ultimately have nothing to offer. They could be rude to you and it is no skin off their nose. If you quit on the spot, the next day they could fill your role. They have no need to be anything more to you than a supervisor that pushes you to do the work.

Who were your leaders that owed you nothing? Which ones did more than push you? Which ones respected you? Did any of them inspire you? Those are the ones you want to emulate. Those are the leaders that really knew what leadership was about. They made you feel like you were part of something larger. They motivated you to be more than what you were and rewarded you when you did well. They were a leader for you even when you had nothing to offer them. That is who you want to be.

Once you know the traits of the kind of leader you want to be, and, even more critically, who you don't want to be, then you have a good idea of who you are. You know your leadership qualities. You know your personal code. When you are faced with a difficult decision or conversation, you not only have the benefit of training and experience to guide you, but you can think back to the leaders that made you who you are and make the best decision for you at that moment. This is how you can sleep at night even when you must make tough calls. Being a leader is hard.

You will have bad days. You will be asked to do things that impact the lives of others. You will make mistakes. But you can carry on when you know who you are and you stay true to those values.

THE 4 TRAITS OF INNOVATIVE LEADERS

Everyone envisions themselves to be a great leader. The person whom an army would follow into battle. Those that watch Star Trek aspire to have the strength of Kirk, the diplomacy of Picard, the tactical prowess of Sisko, and the emotional intelligence of Janeway. All in one neat package. Such goals are admirable, if unrealistic. These fictional leaders have the advantage of knowing the ends before they happen. It is easy to hold firm and deliver a cutting response to your adversary when you read the screenplay and know how they will respond. It's much harder in the real world where the outcomes are unknown.

We cannot see the future. We cannot predict every outcome. We must measure our responses because, unlike television, people don't just bow down when you make a snarky comment. Likely, they will dig in deeper. All we can do is be as prepared as possible. Position ourselves such that we have the best chance of success when those moments arrive. That preparation is what makes great leaders.

Former President Obama once said that he never gets the easy problems. By the time they reach his desk, a dozen or more people have tried to solve it and failed. He is their last hope. As a leader, you need to prepare. You need to learn from your experiences. You need to know who you are. You must always look for the next tool to help you be a better leader. The problems that reach you are the most difficult and you need to be ready.

To get you in the best position to lead, let's look at the 4 traits at the core of all innovative leaders.

Vision

When you drive down the road, you do not look at the hood of your car. Your eyes are not glued to the road just 10 feet in front of you. That is a recipe for disaster. You need to see beyond that. By the time the road reaches your wheels, you've already seen it, analyzed it, and made any required decisions.

Drivers look well in front of the car. They want to see where they are going. Where is the next turn? What obstacles are in the way? Is the road smooth? Is there construction ahead? No good driver would wait until they are at the intersection to make the decision to turn. That decision was made well in advance. The same applies to leadership.

Strategic thinking means you use your peripheral vision to keep tabs on the here and now. You trust your team to keep things moving and make decisions that will keep the business operating. Your attention is meanwhile fixated on what happens in a month or two months or a year down the road. You are playing out the scenarios. You are focused on climate, not weather.

It is vital that leaders NOT get bogged down in the day-to-day minutia of the team. If you find yourself constantly making everyday decisions for the team, then you need to ask yourself why the team is not doing this on their own. Are they not properly trained or are you not trusting them? The leader makes sure the ship gets built. They never tell people how to cut each board.

Inspiration

If the leader is not excited about the plan, then no one else will be either. A leader must be able to rally support. This doesn't necessarily mean you have to be able to deliver rousing speeches to the troops. More than anything, this means you need understand their motivations and concerns and make sure you build a culture that they want to succeed in.

Everyone has their own reason for doing what they do. Some want money. Some want power. Some want recognition. Some want rewards. Whatever it is, a leader needs to know what each person wants and ensure that their contributions are appropriately rewarded. If you have a team member that wants money and all you offer them is an employee-of-the-month plaque, then they will very soon be your former employee. It is up to you know what they want and make it happen.

Another part of inspiration is making sure the team knows that their work has purpose. No one wants to get up at 6am every day and put in a full day's work and then have everything they did get thrown in the trash. They want their work to be praised, to make headlines. They need to hear their VP mention it. In the absence of other rewards, just knowing that their work is important can go a long way. Not everyone that worked on the Apollo missions was an astronaut. Someone had to sweep floors and clean toilets. They did not make headlines, but you can bet that most took pride in what they did because they were a part of something special.

An old Chinese proverb says, "None of us is as strong as all of us."

For all the talk about how certain players carry their teams, football teams still have 11 players on a side. Baseball teams still send a full complement of fielders to the turf even when the star pitcher is on the mound. Pele never ran onto the pitch alone. The best player of all time playing solo against a united team will lose every time.

Leaders inspire the group to work as a unit toward a common goal.

Communication

It is during times of distress that true leaders reveal themselves. Do they throw up their arms and make excuses or do they move forward and find new paths to victory? Do they look for people to blame or take on the work of finding a long-term solution? Do they question every decision that was made or eliminate interference and let the experts do their job? A leader does not need to solve every problem. Instead, they make it possible for others to do so.

Even the best quarterbacks throw interceptions now and then. The team doesn't fold up everything and head to the locker-room. The coach doesn't dwell on it the rest of the game. Problems, and how you deal with them, are what define the kind of leader you are. If you cannot navigate problems, then you will struggle as a leader.

Working through challenges comes down to communication. This can be providing performance feedback, or it can be bringing together a group to focus on finding a solution. It begins with talking through what is needed.

The best leaders are those that do not build silos. They are not concerned about what their team does vs what another team does. They are concerned with moving forward. They value collaboration. They reward those that work with others.

Communication is the tool that can solve most any problem.

Education

A leader is never satisfied with where they

are now. There is always room for improvement. The processes that are groundbreaking today will be obsolete in a year. You must stay ahead of the curve.

Consider the case of Kodak. Formed in 1892, the company became synonymous with personal photography. Kodak's entire business model was built around cameras and film and printing pictures. For nearly 100 years they dominated the market, but they didn't stay in front of the technology.

Despite inventing the digital camera in the 1970s, they continued to push film as the medium for capturing pictures. As a result, when digital cameras took off, Kodak was left in the darkroom and are now little more than a niche company struggling to find a new identity.

Whether it is your own personal development or a trend in the industry, an innovative leader needs to be constantly focused on improvement and what is next. Remember, it is not about doing better at the things you do today, it is about doing better things.

In the following chapters, we will dig into each of these traits even more.

VISION

During the summer of 1787, 55 delegates from 12 states met in Philadelphia to create a new constitution for the United States of America. Over the course of 6 weeks, they debated provisions and reached compromises on many issues.

As they completed the document, they added a preamble to serve as an introduction and guide for future generations.

"We the People of the United States, in Order to form a more perfect Union, establish Justice, insure domestic Tranquility, provide for the common defense, promote the general Welfare, and secure the Blessings of Liberty to ourselves and our Posterity, do ordain and establish this Constitution for the United States of America."

These words are the vision statement for the country. They establish the core principles that the nation is built upon. This vision is what has allowed future generations to correct errors made in the original document. Such visions are critical not just in forming new nations, but in any endeavor that requires unity among a group.

A vision is not a plan. It is not a set of goals, it is a direction. It is standing on the bow of a ship, pointing to the horizon, and saying, "That way." It is a picture of what you want the future to be.

A vision can be small in scope, such as creating a web post that gets people to think. Or it can be large, such as ending discrimination throughout the world. Whatever the dream, the vision is what brings people together.

Leading always starts with a vision. Innovative leaders must know where they want to go. They must be able to inspire others to want to go there too.

Be mindful that a narrow vision forced on others is nothing more than oppression. A worthy vision is one that benefits everyone and unites them to that purpose.

The most successful leaders are able to see beyond today and look to what might be. Visionary leaders are not held back by the here and now or how things used to be. They instead inspire others to a future greater than we ever imagined.

DEFINE YOUR VISION

What is a vision? Why is it important? How do you make one? What about a mission statement? Aren't they the same thing? How much detail should you include? You've barely left port and already the questions seem overwhelming. Where do you even start?

On May 5, 1961, Alan Sheppard became the first American in space. His spacecraft, the Freedom 7, launched on a ballistic trajectory–it did not go into orbit–and the flight lasted just over 15 minutes. Even with this great accomplishment, the United States still trailed the Soviet Union. The USSR had already put a man into orbit a month earlier. Given the tension of the cold war, it was imperative that the United States not fall behind in the race to space.

Twenty days after Alan Sheppard's flight, President Kennedy went before a joint session of congress to address matters critical to the security of the country. Among the items brought up during his speech, President Kennedy made this, now famous, request:

"I believe that this Nation should commit itself to achieving the goal, before this decade is out, of landing a man on the Moon and returning him safely to Earth."

This sentence has been repeated many times as an example of setting a vision. He made a clear goal that was measurable and established something that the country could rally behind. A less quoted comment came later in the address when he noted the anticipated pushback he would receive when asking for the necessary funding for this endeavor:

"For while we cannot guarantee that we shall one day be first, we can guarantee that any failure to make this effort will make us last."

With this address, President Kennedy rallied the country behind this cause and made it clear that finishing last to the Soviet Union was simply unacceptable.

Your team may not have goals as lofty as landing humans on the moon, but every person needs a reason to operate. They need a cause that gets them excited every day. A reason to come to work. And, perhaps most importantly, a beacon that keeps them on track when difficult decisions need to be made.

Imagine you are an engineer working late into the night. You have several projects in motion and must decide what to focus on. You know all are important and you have trouble weighing the options. This is where the vision comes in. It is like the personal code we discussed earlier; a variable that can tip the scales. You are not just flipping a coin, but rather, asking which project moves the needle closer toward the desired end state.

A carefully crafted vision can keep everyone on track and end many debates about priorities.

Before we get into how you create your own vision statement, let's talk about the often-confused Mission Statement. Lots of times people use these two terms interchangeably, but they are quite different. Mission Statements cover what the company/team does, who we do it for, and how we do it. Vision statements cover why.

Let's use Google as an example.

Mission Statement
To organize the world's information and make it universally accessible and useful.

Vision Statement
To provide access to the world's information in one click.

At first glance, you might be saying, "holy crap those sound practically identical," and you would be right. And that is good. If they sounded different then that would mean your vision and your mission are not aligned.

Let's look more closely at the mission. It covers what they do, *organize the world's information.* It covers who they do it for, *universally.* And how they do it, *make it accessible and useful.* In 12 words they cover a lot of ground. They even got double-use out of some words.

We can see the "What", the "Who", and the "How." What about the "Why?"

That is where the vision statement comes in. What is Google's purpose? Why do they exist?

A vision is something that is beyond measure. It is something you ponder whilst standing on a cliff looking out across the ocean. It is the world you long to live in. Access to the world's information in one click.

President Kennedy didn't say how to achieve the goal. He simply pointed to the moon.

Employees can see the vision and understand why they do what they do. People outside the company can read it and say, "wow, I want to work there."

I recommend using Google's universally accessible tool for the organization of the world's information and searching for example vision and mission statements. Every large company has them online. Some are better than others. Read them, break them down. Compare them to your experiences with that company. Does the company do what they say? Are their visions clear? If you were to write your own vision for them, what would it be?

So how do you make one of your own?

My first words of advice are, don't do this in a vacuum. You have a team of people all with their own ideas of where the group is going. Listen to them. You will be surprised at the perspectives. If the team contributed to the vision, they are more likely to embrace it.

These are the core questions you need to ask to get the discussion started.

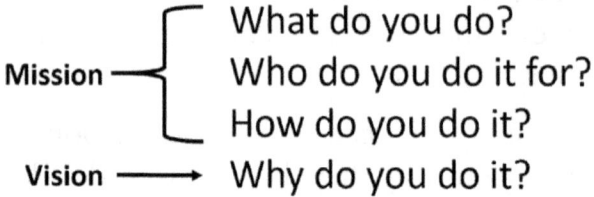

Mission ⟶ ⎰ What do you do?
Who do you do it for?
How do you do it?

Vision ⟶ Why do you do it?

Don't just answer them yourself. Ask your team. Get them to provide their thoughts. See how their ideas differ from yours and others on the team. This can help greatly when you are trying to get alignment later.

Once you have the data, start the conversations. Meet with individuals. Meet with the team. Narrow the focus down to the essence of what your vision should be. Recognize everyone that participates. Make it about the process and the result, not individual ideas.

Craft several drafts of both your mission and your vision. Have the team review them and even put out a poll. It does not have to be a complete democracy. You ultimately get the final say. But getting input from everyone is incredibly engaging and makes later steps much easier.

And, best of all, you now have purpose. You have a reason for the things that you do every day.

ALIGN YOUR VISION

Aligning your vision is akin to the child that wakes up on Christmas morning to find all the gifts that Santa has brought them. Anticipation. Possibility. Excitement that dreams are about to become a reality.

The only question is, where to begin?

When you point your finger to the unexplored lands beyond the horizon and say, "go there," it is typical for the team to start running in a bunch of different directions. Everyone will have their own ideas of what it means and how to get there. You will be bombarded with questions and suggestions and complaints.

No matter how much you involved the team in the planning, some will be openly opposed to the idea. Those that embrace challenges will be ready to swim the ocean themselves. It is important to let each person have their time to process everything. Answer questions but hold off on getting too far into the 'how' part of the conversation. Let the leaders of the team start organizing their thoughts and those of others. Then you can start defining parameters for the journey.

Perhaps the biggest moment in a marketing campaign is the reveal. Every year at the E3 conference, people crowd the halls to see the different companies unveil their latest product. There is a lot of ooing and ahhhing and thousands of pictures are taken. Over the days that follow, reviews of the products will begin to emerge on the internet. Some will tout how wonderful and groundbreaking they are. Others will complain that they are just a derivative works unworthy of your time. Weeks and months will then go by before the products are released to the public. In that time, consumers will form their opinions. When each product is finally released, an entirely new round of reviews, this time from consumers, will make the rounds. The process starts all over again and, if the company is fortunate, lasts until the next year when they release their new version.

On December 3, 2001, Dean Kamen appeared on Good Morning America and unveiled his new invention. In the weeks leading up to this unveiling, hype had grown to a fever pitch. There was a great deal of speculation about what this new technology would be. Dean Kamen had a reputation for innovation, having developed the iBOT Mobility System and the Auto Syringe drug infusion pump. Expectations were high for this new product. Some of the guesses bordered on science fiction.

On that day, he said a few words to Charlie Gibson and Diane Sawyer and then revealed the product. The Segway Personal Transport. There was applause, as you would expect. Charlie and Diane strapped on helmets and went for test rides while others, more trained on the product, demonstrated it around them. In Dean's words, this product was going to revolutionize transportation. He envisioned cities being redesigned around these devices. It would be as revolutionary as the car was.

The public, however, saw it as little more than a glorified scooter. Sure, it had some fancy gyroscopic stabilization device in it that explained the $5,000 price tag, but the collective response from the public was, "ho hum." Over the years we've seen them pop up in police and security departments, and as a novelty for walking tours around historic districts and such. But at best they were a collectible and at worst they were a punchline.

In April of 2015, the company was sold to the Chinese firm, Ninebot, who made them for another 5 years. In June of 2020, Ninebot announced they were ceasing production. Less than 20 years after its unveiling, the device that would revolutionize transportation fizzled out with a whimper.

The Segway unveiling was a textbook example of the type of buzz you want with your vision. You want people excited about it. You want them discussing it. You want everyone tuning in to see it for the first time. What Segway didn't have was a plan for day two.

So how do you prevent your strategy from becoming the next Segway Personal Transport—no doubt NOT the historical legacy Dean Kamen was hoping for on that balmy day in December, 2001.

There are a few key items to focus on.

Make the message about the team

Know your team. What resonates with them? What are they hoping the strategy will be? This is where all those one-on-ones while defining your vision come into play. You should have copious notes from those conversations where you know exactly what their hopes and fears are. Now is the time to use that information to tailor your message to each person. If you do not know these things, then you are shooting in the dark and it is unlikely you will hit the mark.

Give them something they can relate to

A vision will often be interpreted as some pie in the sky idea. It can be hard for those in the trenches to translate this to their day-to-day work. They will simply see it as more marketing mumbo jumbo and turn their attention back to their next task. You need to include examples of specific things that impact them. What are the biggest pain points for the team? Use a specific example of how that challenge will change because of this new strategy.

Focus on the short-term value

Humans have short attention spans. You are paid to think long-term, but they are paid to live in the day-to-day. Bring the message into their realm. Focus on what will happen tomorrow, next week, next month. Be specific about these things. Tie them back to complaints you have heard. What they want to hear is how their life will be better right now.

You often hear about government programs where they talk about how it will save some huge amount of money over the next 10 years. How does that help you? A lot can happen in 10 years. That doesn't help me get more time with my family tomorrow.

Some long-term vision is good, but it only matters if the short-term value is established. Sell them on the short-term view then they will enjoy seeing where this all leads.

Aim high

This is where you give them the big picture. Show them how all this comes together to make a better world. It really helps to be specific about things. Find the biggest pain point and make sure you highlight how once wc gct through this, that work simply goes away. This is something they can relate to and gives them a long-term purpose. Remember, it is built on the short-term objectives.

Connect it to the corporate goals

One of the biggest killers of morale is when people work on something that they think no one cares about. Imagine if your job was to sweep the floor at mission control. No one said a word to you all day or even acknowledged your existence. Now imagine that at the end of the mission wrap-up, you were recognized by leadership for your work in making sure that the engineers had a welcoming environment to work in. Your attitude toward your role changes completely. You need to make sure it is clear to everyone that this vision is directly aligned with where the company is going. Do not be afraid to drop names of leaders that are onboard with this vision and are excited to see it progress each month. If you can get a leader higher up than you to mention this effort (and even some specific names) on the next town hall, you will be golden.

Follow through

If your review with the team is one meeting and then back to business as usual, you have lost. Everyone will simply go back to what they were doing and that will be the end of that. In the first couple weeks, you need to be talking to those that are most welcoming of change. You need to make sure they are on board. You need to meet with those that are absolutely opposed to it and understand their concerns. This needs to be part of the everyday conversation until people forget how it used to be done.

Rolling out your vision is an exciting moment. Aligning it to the expectations of your team and your consumers will ensure that moment becomes something you can build on.

REFINE YOUR VISION

There is an old gag where a company hangs a suggestion box on the wall. It has a slot in the top where employees can drop pieces of paper with their ideas. When you step back, however, you realize that the box is hung directly above a waste basket. Anything dropped in the box goes directly in the trash.

This joke comes from the notion that too often companies and teams do not actually take ideas from the employees into consideration. They give it lip service and act like they care, but when it comes down to it, leadership makes the decisions and whatever the team has to say about it doesn't matter.

You do not want this to be your team.

Getting and using input from your team can

be the difference between reaching your goal and foundering at sea. A great motivating force is the knowledge that you have actual input into the outcome. Everyone wants to see that they are taken seriously, and their ideas are factored into the plan. This cannot be a hand wave. There needs to be genuine interest in their ideas.

Each member of your team is like a member of the intelligence community. The United States has several organizations focused on gathering intelligence on various threats around the world or within the country. The people that make decisions at higher levels use this data to send troops to different locations or to keep an eye on suspicious activity.

Your team is your intelligence department. They are there in the trenches day-in and day-out. No one knows better than them what they are facing. You might think you do, but even if you rose through the ranks from that level, you are not there anymore. You are the officer sitting in your command tent far from the battlefield. To them, you know no more about what they deal with than a citizen at home. They are the ones with the knowledge. If you want honest productive feedback, you need to respect this.

Do not ignore your intelligence community and make the mistake in thinking you know everything. Use them. Ask them. Work with them to solve the challenges.

There are few things you need to do to encourage input and to get value from it.

Provide Guidance

How many times have you been on a team meeting or a town hall where the leader will go through a lengthy presentation about one or more topics and then ask for questions. There is always this awkward moment where no one says anything. Some of this is because people are uncomfortable speaking up in front of others. It is also because they do not know what to ask. What is an appropriate question for that forum? The CEO is not going to be able to answer why there is never any college-ruled paper in the supply cabinet. You want to hold leaders accountable, but the wrong question could get people rolling their eyes at you.

So how do you bridge this gap?

You provide guidance. Without limiting the scope of what they could ask, you offer some areas they might have questions about. For example, you might ask if they have any questions about the methodology or the new alignment that was proposed. Was anyone wondering about the procedural changes that are coming? Offer some possible topics where you have more information you could share. Sure, you could just go into detail about the procedural changes, but if people are more interested in the new methodology, then you are wasting your time. Put it in front of them and let them decide what they want you to cover. Sort of like a "Choose Your Own Adventure" book. Of course, if they have other questions, that is fine too. This is just a means to help get the conversation started.

In a more one-on-one setting, I have an approach that I have used for years that works well for me. I ask the team member, "What are 3 things you would like to see changed on the team?" This lets me know what their biggest concerns are, and gives me the best opportunity to find at least one that will align with something we are going to be doing as part of the new strategy. I can then focus on that item. If they have issues that do not directly align, then I will make note of them and make plans to discuss them more in a later one-on-one after I have a chance to think about it some more.

In any case, people are never just given a blank canvas and asked to fill it in with their thoughts. They have prompts to guide them and get them thinking about it.

Recognition

Those that provide feedback need to be recognized. They need to know that not only was their idea read and considered, but they were rewarded for making the attempt. Let's think about that suggestion box. Often the idea in the real world is that such boxes would be submitted anonymously. People could be free to submit any idea they wanted without fear of any reprisals.

I am forced to ask, what kind of culture do you have if people are scared to offer ideas? That speaks to an even larger problem within the team. The team is most effective when people can say what is on their minds. That doesn't mean we have to agree or support it, but we at least must be appreciative that they contributed.

When the feedback arrives, it should have the person's name on it and those people should be recognized for their contributions both individually and to the group. You could even track contributions monthly and give rewards, if that is appropriate for your team.

You want to build a culture where there is no fear about providing honest and productive contributions, instead such feedback is rewarded.

Consideration

The main part of the gag mentioned earlier is that the box emptied right into the waste basket. No one really cared what anyone had to say. I have talked with a lot of people through my career who have a lot to say in private. Whenever I ask why they don't say something, they respond that no one cares anyway, so why bother. This is frustrating to me and is all too common.

For me personally, I don't care whether anyone cares or does anything with what I say, I will simply feel better knowing that I got it out there. It is cathartic to know that I at least said my peace. If they choose to ignore it, then that is on them. This is why I write to my representatives in congress.

I live in a state that is predominately in a different place on the political spectrum from me. My representatives' opinions on policy decisions are usually very different from my own. I know that when I write to them, I will get a form letter back that says, "Thank you for your letter, here is what we are doing -- usually the opposite of what I wish they would do --, have a nice day." I have no illusions that my letter is going to change the mindset of my representative and that they will suddenly have a seismic shift in their beliefs. But I get it out there. I say what I need to say. If it is an important enough issue, I will write more letters. I might even call. But that is me. Others get too frustrated when they know nothing will happen and choose to just keep it to themselves.

So how do you combat this? Consider that my representative at least sent me a response. They acknowledged that my comments were received. Form letter or not, at least I know my letter didn't go directly to the waste basket. Some staffer had to read enough of it to determine what form letter to send back. That is a start.

But you can do more than that. You are not representing tens of thousands of people. You have a team of three or a dozen. There is no reason you cannot look at each suggestion and provide personal responses back. Your replies do not need to be lengthy reports on the merits of the idea. You simply need to acknowledge that you received the input, thank them for providing it, and give your brief thoughts on what you think about it.

If the suggestion is worthy, make sure it gets on the agenda for the next team meeting. If not, try to find something positive in it and focus on that. If the comment is off in the weeds and you just don't see it, setup some time to talk in more detail to see if there is something you are missing. In all cases, the person will know that you did take the time to read it and are interested in what they have to say. This alone will encourage them to contribute more and will make them feel that the team is what they contribute.

Filter Out the Disruptive Feedback

There is a substantial difference between productive conversation and disruptive accusations. Often people will think that an open environment means they can say anything they want and there is nothing anyone can do about it. They will offer suggestions that are hurtful to others or attack groups or individuals. That is not what we are talking about here. These things have no place anywhere.

If someone cannot offer their idea without attacking a person or group, or without being disrespectful to the team, then that person is the problem.

As an example, imagine the team has a few members that are new and struggling to get up to speed on the new technology. A productive contribution is pointing out that the new technology has a steep learning curve and we need to put a program in place that allows everyone to learn and understand it.

A disruptive contribution is pointing out that the new team members are not pulling their weight. They've had just as much time to learn this as the others on the team and they are not getting it. Maybe they just aren't cut out for this role.

One could argue that the second comment might be accurate. Maybe the new people are not cut out for the role. But how you say something matters. The disruptive comment seeks to demean certain members of the team and place blame for the struggles entirely on their shoulders. The person making the accusation is trying to elevate their standing on the team by diminishing the standing of others. This is not acceptable and should not be tolerated.

When I say that all input needs to be recognized and appreciated, I am referring to productive conversation, not disruptive accusations. Make sure you keep the latter in check.

You will be amazed at how open people are with their ideas when they see that their productive contributions are used to refine the vision for the team.

BUILD A ROADMAP

You've got a vision. You've received feedback. All that is left if to get things done, right? Not exactly.

People struggle to make commitments. They will prefer to focus on what they do best and, when good things happen, take credit for it. But achieving something is only worthwhile if there was a risk associated. Victory is sweeter when the stakes are high. Reaching the summit of Mount Everest is celebrated not just for what it is, but because getting there is a feat that, to this day, can be deadly upon failure. At the same time, if the goals are too high they will seem unattainable and the team might lose interest.

Even with a clear vision and everyone

onboard, it can be a challenge to set goals the team can get behind. Often, goals don't relate to the work a particular individual is doing. They end up doing their job the best they can and hoping it aligns. Another big challenge is that goals are often set at the beginning of the year, and not reviewed again until maybe midyear, or even at the end of the year. People will forget they even had goals.

There are three things that need to be considered when talking about goals.

Input

We covered already the importance of getting input from the team. This is particularly true when it comes to defining the specific goals. They are in the best position to tell you what is possible. The challenge is that people will tend to aim for what they know they can achieve instead of what is possible. They naturally want to set themselves up for success.

In this case, you each have different objectives. They want clearly defined expectations so they can know that they did what you asked. You, on the other hand, want people to challenge themselves to achieve greater things. It can be difficult to bridge this gap.

It starts with conversations. You must understand where they are coming from and identify the true limitations. If you want to completely overhaul the process, but they know from experience that it will take more than a year, then you need to ask them what target is attainable. How much of the process could we get done? Make this a dialogue where you are trying to find what is right, not force your will on others. When you each leave the conversation, you should feel like you have established goals that are both challenging and realistic. And then you repeat this conversation with each person on the team. Compare the notes and repeat until you have a set of goals that the team is happy with.

Naturally, some on the team will still think the goals are too high. Others will feel they are not really changing anything. But as long as they are something the team can get behind, then that is a key step.

SMART

Any search on the internet about setting goals will get into great detail about setting SMART goals. **S**pecific, **M**easurable, **A**ttainable, **R**elevant, and **T**ime-bound. These are good guidelines.

Of course, anything worth having as a

standard is worth expanding on into new standards. So now we have SMARTER, and SMARTTA, and SMARRT to work with as well. After exhausting all variations that play off 'SMART', the industry decided we could use other words like CLEAR and PURE. Then they tossed out the restriction of spelling words entirely and introduced CPQQRT. It is all a little hard to manage. Trying to decide what is right for you can be a bear. I personally think a lot of this is overkill and makes goals more complicated than they need to be.

Think about the terms of service agreements that are ubiquitous on the internet. Specifically, those surrounding behavior on message boards. Some of these terms can be pages and pages of everything that is permitted and not permitted, and how you will be treated if you violate the rules, and on and on. On the other side is the brilliantly brief "Don't be mean"– and other, less euphemistic, variants. Both policies cover the same ground, but the latter sums it all up in just a few words most reasonable people can understand.

There is a greater concern than just brevity: specificity. When you have pages and pages of what you can and can't do, then you get into a situation where, if it is not specifically listed in the document, it will be considered out of scope. You didn't specifically say that people could not post pictures of X. And since you went to great lengths to list out the things you thought were offensive, that would indicate you did not think that X was offensive. By trying to cover everything you are actually opening the door to allow anything else through. But if your criteria is focused on the intent—not wanting people to be mean—then you can be more flexible in the specifics.

Let's bring this back to goals. If I make SMART goals (or some variation) where I am specific about what I want done and when it needs to be done, then I have essentially told the team that I want nothing ELSE done. I set a goal to make our hamburgers the best they can be. The team succeeds, but meanwhile our fries are now the worst in the industry. I didn't say anything about fries in the goal so everyone succeeded, but our restaurant is failing.

For this reason, I like SMART as a guide, but not the be-all, end-all. I want to leave things open for people to exceed expectations. Make it clear that we are rewarded for going above and beyond and for looking at the big picture. Never forgetting our vision.

OKRs

Google uses a different method for Goals that are called OKRs. **O**bjective and **K**ey **R**esults.

The objective is the quality and the key result is the quantity. Both are important in calculating how well we did. The mantra is that if you cannot put a number to it, then it is not a key result.

As an example, "I will make us the most respected burger joint in the country as measured by the positive ratings for our food."

If we know our burgers need to improve, I am not limiting the goal to just that item. Our goal is to be the best across the board. We are measured on the feedback for everything. If we sacrifice one area to excel in another, then we have not won.

OKRs are, by design, high marks. It is not expected that you will hit them. If you can get to 80% of what they state, then you have done very well. We want the team to be challenged. We want them to strive to do more. We want them to focus on the big picture. We want to be specific without being specific.

Regular Review

A recurring theme in this book is the need for constant communication. Everything that you do only means something if you are talking about it so much that it is part of the culture. If you have a meeting about goals and everyone nods their head and then you do not mention the goals again until end of year evaluations, then people will not even remember they had goals. You never made them part of the culture.

What is important to your team is the things that you talk about regularly. If you don't mention it, then you must not care about it.

OKRs should be shared, and then discussed, in every team meeting and every one-on-one. They should be put on a dashboard for all to see. People should know exactly where THEY stand on meeting those goals. They should be what everyone's day revolves around. The whole idea is that these goals are what we need to do to achieve the vision, so they should be part of the everyday work.

If the goals are a burden to the work, then something is broken. That means we have set goals that are not aligned with the work we do. That is a problem. Knowing that early in the cycle is what allows us to fix it.

Do not be in a position where you never talk about the goals all year and realize in November that the team didn't accomplish what they set out to do. You want to know that in March so you can refine the OKRs in April and get back on track. If a person is struggling to achieve their goals in April, then that conversation needs to happen in April so they have time to correct it.

This communication is what keeps everyone focused on the goals and improving the team. And it will make your job easier as a leader, because then when you are asked by your leadership what you accomplished this year, all you need to do is pull up the dashboard for your goals and send them the details.

INSPIRATION

Near the end of the 1996 film *Independence Day*, humanity is readying to mount an assault on the invading aliens. President Whitmore jumps up on a truck and gives a rousing speech about the importance of what they are about to do and how proud everyone should be. The music swells and the crowd cheers, ready to fly into battle.

While this is a great scene, it is nothing like the kind of inspiration that leaders in the real world will need to practice. Inspiration is not an exciting speech or any singular moment. Inspiration is more personal. It is making a connection with individuals every day.

Moving speeches are like sprints. The effects

are short-lived. Within an hour, people will have moved on. By the end of the day, they mostly forgot you had even spoken. True inspiration needs to be a marathon. It is a long process of working with people to keep them on track.

Inspiration requires that you recognize your role in the effort and work closely with people to make sure they are getting what they need. You might need to give the occasional speech to ignite a spark, but don't rely on those. They burn out fast. You need the embers that you have placed along the way to keep moving forward.

INSPIRATION VS MOTIVATION

On December 7, 1941, Pearl Harbor was attacked, pulling the United States into the Second World War. This was a defining moment in our history and tens of thousands of citizens were ready to take up the call and go fight for freedom. All of them were inspired to defend their country and save the world.

Three years later, the allies stormed the beaches of Normandy and began making steady progress toward liberating Europe. Soldiers that had signed up with enthusiasm after Pearl Harbor were now worn down and struggling to go on. The horrors they had experienced were taking a toll.

From stories told in the years that followed,

what kept them going was each other. The bonds with other soldiers. Each man did their job because they knew the person next to them was depending on them. They were motivated to do their best because they needed the best from everyone else in order to survive.

The inspiration of saving the world was still there, but it was the motivation of being there for their comrades that got them through each day.

Skip forward a couple decades to the middle of the Vietnam war. This was a conflict started in the name of protecting the world from the spread of communism. Men were drafted and sent to foreign soil to engage in a campaign of attrition.

As with World War II, the men were motivated by each other. That bond kept them going each day. What was missing was inspiration. The cause of defending against communism was abstract. There was no Pearl Harbor moment that brought everyone together. To many, it was simply a war that someone higher up decided needed to be fought.

The war dragged on and claimed the lives of more than 58,000 Americans, but we eventually left and lost the peninsula to communism.

To be your best, you need to be both inspired by the work you are doing and motivated to do that work every day. The dream of putting a man on the moon may be why you took the job at mission control, but it does not put food on the table each night.

Each person on your team is there because they believe in the vision. They stay because they are kept motivated to do their best.

A team that is inspired, but unmotivated, will quickly get frustrated because they desperately want to reach that final goal but find themselves frustrated with the day-to-day work. A team that is motivated, but uninspired, will get burnt out as they slog through the daily grind with no purpose.

The motivation for each person is different. Money. Awards. Status. Promotion. Accolades from leaders. What causes each person to get out of bed in the morning is what you need to find out and provide to them.

There is an episode of the TV show Friends where Rachel is working at the coffee house and frustrated that her desired career in fashion is not happening. She is convinced by Chandler that the reason for her lack of progress is because she does not have 'the fear.' She is too comfortable with where she is and therefore is not putting all the effort needed toward a career in fashion. As a result, she quits her job at the coffee house and goes full speed ahead toward finding a job in fashion.

She knew what she wanted but did not have the proper motivation to get there.

The same is true for each person on a team. They will join your company and your team because they are inspired by the cause. This can be the opportunity to work with a new technology, or with a certain person, or because of the reputation of the company itself. That gets them in the door.

Day-in and day-out, this vision alone will not keep them motivated. Everyone has other things that get them out of bed in the morning.

This can be financial rewards. It can be industry recognition. It can be joy of a great group of coworkers. It can be complete satisfaction in the product they are delivering. Whatever it is, THAT is their motivation. That is what they need or else they will move on to something else.

There are 3 things you can do you to make sure each person is motivated.

Identify it

You need to talk with each person and find out what motivates them. What gets them out of bed in the morning? What drives them to excel? Where are they going in their career? It will be different for each person, and it will likely change over time. The college graduate on day one will have different motivation two years later when they get engaged and start a family. You must keep pace and adapt.

Lean into it

Your motivation will be completely different from theirs. They might very well tell you that they are motivated 100% by financial reward. They want to be paid well or they stay at home. To you, motivated by higher purpose, this sounds selfish. It is not. It is simply different.

Whatever their motivation, you need to embrace it and figure out what you can do to make sure they get it. I am not saying that you need to go over the top and pay those people more than you would others, but you need to be sensitive to the fact that they are driven by money. If the annual salary budget is not great in some years, you need to make sure your conversation with that person covers how you understand that this is a problem for them, and how you hope that they see this as a bump in the road that they can overcome and not something that causes them to jump ship.

Keep the inspiration

'America' has been a part of global culture for a long time. I am not talking about the country. I am talking about the idea. The notion that you can start with nothing an end up with all the wealth you could imagine. America is a concept of freedom and possibility. It is what large groups of immigrants followed to reach their dreams. "Bring me your tired, your poor, your huddled masses yearning to breathe free. I lift my lamp to you." This is the idea of America. It is inspirational. It is welcoming. It makes you want to go there.

Whatever problems the United States has, that beacon of hope still shines in the harbor to remind us of what the vision of this country is.

You must remind your team why they joined. There will be difficult days. There will be times when the motivation just isn't there. As long as they still see the light that inspired them, they can carry on through those rough spots.

SUPERVISOR VS MANAGER VS LEADER

This is a part of leadership that is often the most misunderstood.

Let's get right into it and talk about what each role is.

A **supervisor** is focused on tasks. Things need to get done and the supervisor is there to ensure that they get done. The best example of this is an assembly line. This is a group of people who each have a singular task to perform. They must perform their task quickly and accurately so as not to hold up the production of the line and to ensure the products being made are of good quality.

The supervisor ensures that the work gets

done. The shift starts and the supervisor walks the line keeping an eye on the activities. If anyone has trouble, the supervisor gets them assistance, or even temporarily replaces them so that the overall production does not fail. They must make sure each person is trained to do the job for the station they are working. For 8 hours, they execute those tasks, and the supervisor is who makes sure it continues without interruption.

But people do not just show up and do a job. How do people know when to be there? How are people hired? How do you assess performance? What happens when someone calls in sick? This is where the manager comes in.

A **manager** is concerned with the operation of the unit. They ensure that the supervisor has the tools needed to perform the tasks. The manager will hire new workers and establish a framework for the schedules. They setup processes for what to do when someone calls in sick. They oversee the team. At the end of the day, the manager is who answers to leadership about how productive the team was, or why there were problems, or any number of other questions they may have. They may not know the specifics of how to screw together a mounting plate on to the frame arm, but they know it is necessary to be successful and will be able to speak to it up the line.

You might think that all bases are covered now, but then we must recall the inspiration vs. motivation conversation from earlier. A manager can motivate the supervisor by providing the rewards that are valuable to them. A supervisor can motivate their workers by doing the same. But where is the inspiration? Where is the reason we do the work in the first place? That is where the leader enters the picture.

A **leader** needs to understand each person and have a clear vision for the team. An assembly line is not merely a group of people doing repetitive tasks all day. It is a team of people working together to achieve a common goal. The leader is who helps them see that.

Each of these roles are critical to the success of a team. You need to have a vision and reiterate that vision to the team. You need to manage the resources and setup processes. And you need to make sure that specific tasks get done. This is not necessarily 3 different people. In most companies, the same person will wear all 3 hats.

The key is to wear the right hat at the right

time. If the only hat you have is supervisor, then your team will accuse you of micro-managing, because you will constantly be all up in their business. You must set them up for success and let them go. But if you are constantly watching every single task they perform and critiquing them on it, then they will get frustrated. Just imagine how difficult it will be to work if your boss was sitting in a chair beside you all day.

So, you need to step back. You need to have confidence in the training you provided and the abilities of the people on your team. You must trust them. If you do not have that trust, then you need to figure out where the problem is and make corrections. The solution is never to hold their hand all day.

Once you have the team trained and the process is running, then your supervisor role is complete. You now step into the manager role.

At this point you are watching things from afar. You are concerned with output. You are concerned with quality. You are concerned with cohesion. There are certainly measures that go back to one individual's performance, but you are not concerned about each action and judging it, you are looking at the whole. This is climate, not weather. The events of a single day do not define the team. What is the trend? What are the anomalies? Those are what you are concerned about as a manager. There will be times when you need to put on that supervisor hat and step in to deal with a situation, but only when necessary.

Now the team is operating on all cylinders. People know their roles and their tasks and the processes. They need less management. They need a leader.

A leader is there to answer the question, "Where are we going?" Sure, we are building contraptions and boxing them up and shipping them to customers, but next year we will have to build a new contraption and we will have to do it faster. How will we do that?

Get that leadership hat on. You need to be thinking several steps ahead of where the team is today. You need to be putting programs in place that set the team up for future success. The manager is concerned about today's operations, but you as the leader are looking to tomorrow and beyond.

You setup a program to cross-train each person so they can work multiple positions. You look at career development information from each person, and see there are several people that want to be supervisors. So, you train them to fulfill that role and cover for the actual supervisor when they are out. You see a report from another department where next year we are bringing in a new tool to speed up delivery. You need to make sure people have the training on this tool and reassure them that this tool is not meant to eliminate jobs, but rather make them more productive.

As a leader, your view of the day-to-day operations is only through your peripheral vision. You know what is going on. You know if things are good or bad. But you let your manager handle the everyday details. You are focused on the future. You are building the new vision and strategic plan.

Each of these roles is important and critical to the operation of the team. We already covered how if someone is only a supervisor, they will have a team that is frustrated and unhappy. The same goes for the leader role. If you only do the leadership tasks, then you will be so far removed from the day-to-day activity that the team might not even know who you are. They will see you as someone that does not understand what actually happens in the trenches. You need to know when to wear each hat and never ignore one.

Remember, it is unlikely that there will be

three clearly defined job positions called supervisor, manager, and leader. You will likely be all three and need to know when to where each hat.

BUILD A TEAM OF LEADERS

When you first start on your journey, the team will be trying to figure out their role. Most will be satisfied in simply having a part to play. As you move forward, people will get comfortable in their role and will look to expand their skills. Embracing this is perhaps your most important function as a leader. You should have the goal of building a team of leaders.

A common expression heard in leadership circles is, "lead from every seat." This translates to: you can be a leader no matter what role you have. The college intern can be a leader, just like the seasoned veteran. Neither of them has a title of supervisor or manager or leader, but they can lead just the same.

First of all, why is this important? If you need people to do tasks, then what is wrong with having expertly trained people doing that work? The answer is nothing. You want experts and you need experts. The key is that you do not want people so heads-down invested in their work that they do not see the big picture.

Going back to the conversations about vision, you need people that understand WHY they are doing what they are doing and can convey that to others. This is what allows them to make appropriate decisions when obstacles are encountered. The last thing you want is for the team to collectively turn their heads to you every time they reach a fork in the road.

There is an old story I heard from my father. It refers to a man working in a factory. Someone comes up to this man and asks, "What do you do, Joe?" To which Joe responds, "I push the button." His friend, not getting the detail he was looking for, asks his question differently. "What do you MAKE Joe?" To which Joe replies, "I make the push."

Joe was well trained to push the button. He did it well and was proud of his work. But he clearly had no idea even what the button did. He was just told to push it and that was that. If anything went awry, Joe would not be positioned to add any additional value.

In my early years working as a Unix System Administrator, I was often on-call. This was in the days before cell phones were common. Instead, I carried a pager. Remote access was also not nearly as reliable as it is today. Getting a call often meant driving into the office.

The company had an on-site operations team that monitored systems 24x7. When something would occur that flagged an alert, this team was the first to triage the event. They had some basic processes that they could follow to try and resolve the situation on their own. If those steps failed, then they would page the on-call for further assistance. Most of the operators did a great job and were sincerely interested in learning about the systems they were monitoring. There was, however, one operator that was a thorn in my side.

This operator showed no desire to do more than stop the red light from flashing. When he would page me, I would provide some feedback and offer some steps he could take. This was always met with resistance, and I would be told that I needed to come in and get it resolved. I would drive 30 minutes into work, fix the problem in 30 seconds, and drive 30 minutes back home. All because this person did not want to grow outside their bubble. The impact, aside from my loss of sleep, was that while they were refusing to take actions to resolve the issue themselves, the customer was experiencing an outage of some sort. To this person, they did not want any responsibility beyond getting the alert to stop flashing. The fact that a customer was impacted was not a concern of theirs.

This is the problem of not having leaders on the team. If all you do is push a button, then you have no investment in what the group is doing, and you are actually hurting the team.

There are a few traits you need to build a team of leaders.

Trust

You must trust each person on the team to make the right decisions. Spell out the vision. Build your core values. Set your goals. Share your roadmap. And then put your trust in the team.

This does not mean you are at their mercy, but you need to allow each person to make decisions about the things that affect them. Resist the temptation to give each person a specific playbook to execute. Let them build the playbook.

Don't be afraid to fail

Even with excellent alignment to the vision, each person will have a different perspective. The decisions will be different. Their decisions will sometimes be wrong. Your decisions will sometimes be wrong. You must be okay with this and not criticize incorrect decisions that were made with the best of intentions. Learn from the experience, praise the initiative that was shown, and move on.

Focus on what went right

A fact of life in the IT world, and likely others, is we regularly review incidents that occurred. We review them to see what decisions were made and where things went awry. I am all about learning from mistakes, but why do we only focus on what went wrong? Where are the daily meetings to talk about what went right?

We talk all the time about the problems that occurred over the course of a day, and we force the people involved to explain themselves. But couldn't we learn at least as much from the work that was completed without a problem? Instead of asking what went wrong, couldn't we ask what went right?

There was a study done during WWII where Abraham Wald reviewed the damage done to planes that returned from air raids. As planes would return to base, the researchers would draw a sketch of the plane and indicate where it had sustained damage. The sketches were then combined to see the most common areas that sustained damage. In reviewing the data, the military concluded that they needed to increase the armor in these areas. Wald disagreed.

His argument was that these planes returned to base. They didn't need more armor in these locations because clearly the planes took damage and were still able to return home. It is the areas on those planes that showed no damage that needed to be improved. Since none of the planes that returned had damage in those other areas, then those planes must have been unable to return.

Make sure you are looking at the right data so you don't learn the wrong lesson.

If you have established leaders across your team, then they will feel more invested in the work they are doing, they will appreciate that you are looking out for their career development, and you will be better positioned to handle the rough patches.

ENCOURAGE PEOPLE TO LEAVE

Turnover is often used as a measure of a team's quality. During an interview, it is common for a candidate to ask why a position is open. If the team is a revolving door, then that is seen as a red flag. It can, however, be misleading.

Turnover can certainly be an indicator of an unstable team where people get burnt out and leave. But it could also be an indicator of a team that does an excellent job developing people for greater things.

Let's say you take a job loading power supplies into boxes. You are trained and you do a good job. You get good reviews and even earn a pay raise or two. But you never load anything else into the boxes. You never take on any additional responsibilities. This might be fine and maybe you are content with this arrangement. Great. But what if you are not okay with it? What happens then?

You spend a year loading power supplies and you see a job opening on another team or with another company and they need someone that can load keyboards into boxes. You go and interview, but are rejected because your only experience is loading power supplies. You go to your supervisor and ask if you can get experience loading other parts. They tell you that you are awesome at loading power supplies, and they really need you where you are. You go back to your job and try to make the best of it.

You think about your career some more and realize that there are several assembly lines where people load power supplies. If you could work toward being a supervisor for these people, then that would be a nice career step. You go to your supervisor again and ask about training to be a supervisor. They nod their head, but never say another thing about it. You ask again and again, but nothing ever comes of it. Eventually a job comes along at another company where they need a power supply loader. You interview and are offered the job. During your exit interview you are asked why you decided to leave. You respond that there was no career growth.

The supervisor in this scenario was so focused on the day-to-day supervisor tasks, they never put on their leader hat to make sure the team members were getting out of the job what they wanted. The numbers were being met and that was all that mattered. If this was happening with every position on the assembly line, then the turnover rate would be extremely high. Every month there would be more people leaving for other jobs because this team was a dead end.

Let's change the scenario just a little. What if that supervisor agreed to let you train in other areas? Soon you would be knowledgeable on loading all kinds of stuff. Then you ask to be trained as a supervisor. They give you training, send you to some classes, and even ask you to cover for them when they take a day off. You see a supervisor position open up on another team and you jump at the chance. Your supervisor gives you a great recommendation and you get the job.

In both cases, the supervisor has lost one of their team members, but the circumstances were completely different. In one case, you have a team of people that are locked into a singular role and care only about executing the task. They have no prospects for anything greater on this team. In the other case, you have a team made of people that are constantly expanding their knowledge and experience. They are excited in the work and take pride in accomplishing more. They are owners of the team. They care for the team because you care for them.

I tell my team members all the time that I am perfectly fine with them pursuing jobs outside of my team. I would prefer that they move up within the company, but part of my goal is to get them to advance in their career. It serves no one if I were to hold them back.

Make sure you put on your leader hat when needed. During employee check-ins, you need to know exactly what each person is after. You need to provide guidance on how they can get there. That is how you build loyalty. If you create an environment where people are positioned to go anywhere, it is more likely that they will prefer to stay where they are. Not necessarily on your team, but in the company. And that makes the company stronger.

COMMUNICATION

A question often posed in the world of philosophy is, "If a tree falls in the woods and no one is around to hear it, does it make a sound?" How do you measure the impact of something that is not observed? We can only discuss events and assess their impact if we are aware of them.

Communication is at the heart of all recognition, feedback, and problem resolution. We cannot hope to improve if we are not aware of what needs to be improved. We cannot recognize outstanding work if we are not aware that it occurred.

The best way to ensure that everyone is engaged is to be completely transparent about what is going on. If they are doing well, say so. If they need to work on something, point it out. If the team is coming up short in an area, don't sugarcoat it. If the team had a major win, celebrate it.

Build a culture where open communication is not only encouraged but recognized as an outstanding behavior. Reward those that get outside their bubble and help others. Set an example for everyone that information should be freely exchanged.

Innovation requires the free flow of ideas. We can only do that if we put everything out on the table.

CHECK-IN REGULARLY

As a rule, speaking with their leader tends to make people nervous. Annual performance evaluations are particularly stress-inducing for many. The more stressful it is for the employee, the more likely it is that the leader did not have good communication with the individual during the year. If a leader was effectively communicating during the year, then the end of year evaluation would simply be another conversation and there would be no reason to be nervous.

Most people like to get constructive feedback that points out where they can improve. There are those few who already feel they are perfect, and so any suggestions for improvement will be rejected as your character flaw, but those individuals are the exception. If you present feedback in the right way, then people will appreciate your commitment to their improvement.

Check-ins are a great way to ensure you make midcourse corrections before they become a problem. They allow your team to hear your voice so you can build a relationship with them. This makes them more comfortable and makes the conversations much easier.

So, what is a check-in?

This is something that confuses many. What exactly do you talk about? Are they formal reviews of performance? Are they conversations about goals? Is it for career development? Do you just shoot the breeze? The answer is yes. It is all these things.

Let's go through some key elements to a successful check-in.

Scheduled

You need to put them on the calendar. I stress that you need to do it. Do not expect the team member to do it. People are extremely sensitive to their leaders' time and will hesitate to block off time for this conversation, even if they see open slots on the calendar. You, as the leader, need to put it out there at a time that works for both of you.

And you need to stick to this time. If you need to reschedule one occasionally, that is fine. If you need to cancel one because of vacation time or something, that is okay too. But those need to be the exceptions. The team member must know that you think the conversations are important. If you reschedule them, or cancel them, or simply do not show up for them on a regular basis, they will see that you are not taking it seriously, so they will not take it seriously.

Agenda

As with any meeting, you need to have a plan for what you will discuss. You may not have a formal set of topics for each session, but you need to establish some general topics that are always there. Think of these like writing prompts. They are agenda items; if no one has anything else, you can always go to one of these pre-selected topics. I usually have career development, goal updates, and administrative items as the core topics for the agenda. If I get into a check-in and did not have anything specific, I can always go to career development and ask how they are doing on training, or if there is anything they need to help with some new area of development. These can get the conversation going and often lead to deeper discussions about the team and strategy.

Frequency

This could go with scheduling, but it is important enough that it needs to be its own category. The idea that we set goals in January and then do an annual performance review at the end of the year is a recipe for disaster. You never launch a ship and then cast it across the ocean hoping that your aim was true. You make course corrections to account for wind and seas and other obstacles that get in the way.

These check-ins need to be weekly, if possible, but bi-weekly at a minimum. Your team needs to hear your voice. They need to know that they have your ear regularly. You need to be able to talk to them about things they did well and things that need improvement before they are forgotten.

One-on-One

Do not hold these check-ins as a group. These are not team meetings. These are not town halls. These are private sessions between you and your team member to review items specific to them. Even if you are talking strategy, you are talking about how it impacts them. They need a forum where they can ask you questions that they are hesitant to ask in front of others. Block off the time for them and them alone.

Casual

Nothing says that these need to be uptight discussions. There is no parliamentary procedure required. You have an agenda that you go through, but you should strive to keep the conversation light. This is you and a team member talking. Try to take off the supervisor, manager, and leader hats and just talk to them.

This is also your opportunity to get to know your team members better. They are people with families and lives and personal challenges. Do you know if they are married? Do they have kids? Where are they going on vacation? What big events are coming up? Don't pry if they seem hesitant to share details, but don't be afraid to squeeze in questions of a more personal nature and make notes for yourself so you can follow-up on those things next time. If they had a vacation to Europe planned, ask them how it was the next time you talk to them after they return. Just the fact that you remembered will go a long way toward building a better relationship.

Listen

Whatever you want to get through during the conversation, remember that this is about their career and improvement. It is about them sharing their concerns and questions. Be an active listener that hears what they are saying and asks excellent follow-up questions. You do not have to be Mr. Fix-It that has an answer for everything. It is perfectly fine to simply say, "I don't know." Ask them what they would like to see. Pull information from them. This will help you improve as well. This is what makes you a leader the team respects.

The key take-away in this is constant communication. Build relationships with each person. Show them you care and listen to their concerns. They will understand that you cannot solve everything and that some things are just the way it is. But the fact that you empathize with them will make all the difference and build a much stronger team and make those end-of-year conversations much less stressful for everyone.

PERFORMANCE PROBLEMS (GROUP)

There will be times when the team seems to be firing on all cylinders yet still can't hit any targets. Incidents are too high. Deadlines are being missed. Quality is not where it needs to be. In these cases, morale can take a huge hit.

Navigating these rough patches requires you to focus on three things.

Get back to the fundamentals

The fundamentals of football are blocking and tackling. When a team struggles in a game, the coaches will ground everyone in these fundamentals. Whatever else might happen, make sure you execute your blocks and make solid tackles.

What are your fundamentals? What is the core value your team provides? What are the most basic tasks you are responsible for? Is it packaging widgets? Is it delivering new servers? Is it processing status reports? Whatever it is, do it.

In the movie Apollo 13, there is a scene where Gene Kranz has gathered the engineers together and they are debating all the problems they are seeing. Each person has an idea on what is going on and how to fix it. After some back and forth, he reframes the discussion with the statement, "What do we have on the spacecraft that's good?"

In that moment, he was returning to fundamentals. Whatever else they had planned, right now their focus is simply on keeping this ship functioning. You must do the same.

Identify what your core value is and be willing to sacrifice all other gains so that you can complete those basic tasks. Doing so will lead you to step two.

Adjust your goals

Getting back to the fundamentals means that you need to shift your expectations. The football team is no longer aiming for a touchdown, they just want a first down—or maybe simply a pass completion. Mission control is no longer aiming for the moon, they simply need the ship stabilized. Identify your small victory.

Maybe your goal now is just to get 50 widgets packed without missing any. Or maybe you need one particular server delivered tomorrow. Or maybe that TPS report needs to get to the CEO. Whatever it is, that is your goal. Achieve that and you have won this battle. Then you can look to the next battle. Soon the original goal starts to come back into focus.

Celebrate what you have accomplished

It can be easy when times are tough to feel you are failing. Each setback can feel like you are having to start over. Make sure you never forget the parts of the journey you have already completed. Make sure everyone on the team still feels valued.

How have your individual team members improved? What are they doing better? Recognize individuals for their achievements. Find every success you can and play it up as much as possible. Make the team feel good about what they've done.

Don't get bogged down in the fact that the lofty goals are still eluding you. Get back to basics. Focus on the smaller achievements. Celebrate each victory.

Keep morale high and things will improve.

PERFORMANCE PROBLEMS (INDIVIDUAL)

For the most part, people want to do a good job. They will try their best and accept feedback and strive to continuously improve. It is their career after all, so they have a vested interest in doing well. As a result, most performance problems can be easily addressed with some basic feedback, and coaching, and follow-through.

I will talk a little more about that later, but I first want to talk about the edge cases. There are two performance problems that will suck the energy out of a team very quickly which need to be dealt with aggressively.

The Narcissist

Some team members are self-anointed experts. They have complete confidence in their abilities and look down upon everyone else. They do not need feedback or coaching because they are already in complete command of everything they need. In fact, if you were to imply that they were anything less than perfect they would have no problem telling you that you are incorrect. All they require, and often demand, is your unqualified praise.

These folks can be the worst team members. They will rarely listen to input from others, since they already know the best way to complete every task. They will not share how they solved problems because they think others likely wouldn't understand. You will find that others on the team avoid talking to these individuals.

On the surface, these team members seem invaluable. But the damage they are doing can be irreparable if ignored for too long.

There are two types of narcissists.

1. Those that are actually experts in the field, but they know it and expect everyone else to worship them

2. Those that are nowhere near as good as

they claim to be

A Type-1 narcissist can be the more difficult to deal with, because they are actually providing value. Their knowledge is legit, and you might rely on them to work through issues. But this does not excuse behaviors that poison the team.

Your challenge with these individuals will be in getting them off their pedestal and working with the rest of the team in a productive manner. You will need to give them projects that require collaboration and set some specific goals to track their work. Make it clear that this project is not about just completing the work. It is about HOW they complete the work. During check-ins, ask them questions about their collaboration and what input they took from the team. Send out 360 feedback requests to others on the team to get their feedback.

A Type-2 narcissist is a faux expert. They will "talk the talk" but rely on smoke and mirrors to advance their career.

The best way to deal with them is to ask probing questions during check-ins. When they say they completed a task, ask them to show their work. Demonstrate the code. Explain the report. Force them to prove that they actually understood what they delivered. Give them time-bound goals that can be easily measured and make sure that you always ask follow-up questions.

Unfortunately, narcissists are not the only personality that can be trouble for a team.

The Weak Link

The weak link is the person who just is not pulling their weight. The rest of the team packs ten boxes and they pack four. Not once, but over and over. The rest of the team gets frustrated as they need to pick up the slack, yet somehow this person hangs around.

As with the narcissist, the weak links come in two flavors.

1. Those that CAN'T

2. Those that WON'T

Those that **can't** have all the best intentions. They get in early. They stay late. They read the manuals. They ask for help. They get involved. But no matter what they do, they just don't seem to get it. They are in over their head and maybe this job simply isn't for them.

Your patience can only go so far. The team will get really frustrated if they must keep covering for someone else. Once the person has reached the point where they should be well trained, you need to draw some lines in the sand.

Start with the most basic tasks. Set clear goals. If they succeed, then move on to progressively more complex tasks until you hit a wall. At that point you need to decide if that level of performance is sufficient. If it is, then make sure they know that they will be stuck here unless they can improve. If it is not, then you need to make a difficult decision.

Those that **won't** are, in some ways, the easiest performance problem to deal with. If someone simply does not want to do the job, then it is easy on your conscience to let them go. Set some clear goals. Draw a line in the sand. Engage with HR. Make the call. If someone doesn't want to do the work or learn the work, then they have no place on the team.

It has been said many times that you need to always have something nice to say. Don't just focus on the negative. Always bring in some good things and share those as well.

I want to give a warning about this. This does not mean soften the blow on the things you are concerned about. You need to be direct and specific. It is fine if you want to talk about how they do a great job pushing the green button before you get into their problems with the blue button. What you don't want to do is make it sound like the blue button is not really a problem. You need to come right out and tell them, "Your performance on the blue button is not acceptable and we need to find a way to improve it." No ambiguity. The performance is bad. This sentence gives them the direct message about the problem.

Whatever the performance problem is, the tactics are the same. Set some goals. Set a timeline to reach those goals. Check-in with them regularly. Give them every opportunity to succeed and then make a decision.

Performance problems are where you earn your stripes as a leader. You need to keep everyone motivated to do a good job, while at the same time telling some of them they are doing a bad job. The way you have this conversation is critical. If you screw this up, then that person might well check out and just get frustrated with the job and then it is a lost cause. If you do it right, then they might find the key they needed to make it right and get back on track.

DEALING WITH EXTERNAL FACTORS

On December 31, 1988, the Philadelphia Eagles traveled to Chicago to face off against the Bears in a playoff game. Both teams were winners of their respective divisions. The winner of this game would advance to the NFC championship game.

The teams battled it out on the field with the Bears taking the advantage. With about 2 minutes left in the first half, a fog rolled into part of Chicago and descended on the stadium. This fog lingered through the second half of the game. The fog was so thick that passes more than a few yards down the field became impossible. The TV crew had to resort to sideline cameras to see anything. While the teams combined for 26 points in the first half, the fog limited them to a combined 6 points in the second half. Any preparation the teams had done before the game had to be rewritten on the fly.

As a leader, you will no doubt have numerous plans for different scenarios. You have a strategic plan. You have incident response plans. You have disaster recovery plans. You have daily processes. These are all attempts to prepare for the worst-case scenarios that you might encounter. In the end, however, you cannot plan for everything. Football teams do not have plans for an unexpected fog to roll over the stadium.

Earlier I spoke about the story of Joe and how he made his living pushing the button. He knew not what the button did or why he did it other than he was told to do so. To properly deal with external factors you need to have a team that is built around a full understanding of the goals and not just the execution of a step-by-step plan.

Each person on the team must own the vision and be able to make decisions that lead the team in the right direction. If the ship encounters a storm, you don't wake the captain to decide what to do. Those on the bridge assess the situation, recognize the overall goals, and make decisions based on that situation.

There are three parts to being prepared for the unexpected.

Vision

We've covered vision at length in prior chapters. It is a common theme to leadership. Everyone on your team MUST know where you are going. When you are approached with questions, you need to always consider which decision best fits with the strategic goal. Put everything in those terms so that the team is comfortable thinking that way. Everything you do revolves around that vision. If ever you encounter a scenario where you don't think the vision applies, then either your vision is not well-formed, or you are not approaching the problem correctly.

Flexibility

Expect the unexpected. You need to recognize that things will not go according to plan. I've had people on my team who functioned much better when they were given a plan and told to execute it. They wanted to know what they had to do each day and they would do it perfectly. They were not to the level of Joe the button pusher, but they struggled when they were thrown curve balls. You need to condition your team to not get flustered when these situations arise. It is normal. It is expected. It is sometimes welcomed.

Years ago, I was having a conversation with a senior leader at my company. There was an outage that needed to get resolved and we were having trouble getting the system stabilized due to complexities with the recent patch set. During this discussion I mentioned the difficulties of managing these patches in this environment. His response to me was simply, "If it were easy, anyone could do it." This stuck with me from that moment on. It is true. Everyone on the team is paid to deal with the hard problems. If everything was easy and according to plan, then they would not need us around.

Pilots aren't there to take-off and land in perfect weather and clear skies. They are there to safely fly the plane during storms and when something breaks. Everyone on your team needs to recognize that challenges are part of life, and it is okay when the plan falls apart and you need to come up with a new plan.

Adaptability

Once the team has taken a few breaths and

is okay with the idea of dealing with this new problem, what do you do? You need to be able to come up with alternative solutions. This is where a trained workforce comes in. The reason pilots know how to deal with an engine failure is because they have been trained on the workings of every part of the plane. They know it inside and out.

We are not training Joe to push the button. We are training Joe to build a machine. Soldiers must be able to completely disassemble their guns and put them back together quickly. They must be able to do it blind-folded. They must be able to do it under pressure. This is what allows them to not panic when something breaks. If the gun jams, they are not at the mercy of calling 'gun support' in the middle of a battle. They have the knowledge to adapt to the situation and fix it themselves.

Look at your team. Look at who does what. Do you have specialists? Does the team tend to send certain work to those people? Are people being pigeonholed? That is a problem. You need to cross train. You need to ensure that everyone knows everything that is going on. That does not mean that everyone will be an expert in everything, but everyone will understand everything.

Shortly after the launch of Apollo 12 on November 14, 1969, the spacecraft was struck by lightning. There were instrument malfunctions, and the entire mission was put in jeopardy. While Mission Control scrambled to figure out what to do, Engineer John Aaron recalled something he had seen years before. He relayed the instruction to the crew to "Set SCE to aux."

Some were unaware what this even was, but Alan Bean on the ship knew and he flipped the switch. Everything was restored and the mission was saved.

John Aaron was familiar with the goals of the mission. He was flexible and did not panic when an external factor impacted the execution. He adapted quickly because he had the training in the assorted systems, so he was able to make the connection between the symptoms they were experiencing and the operation of the systems on the craft.

If you can instill these same values in your team, then you will be well positions to deal with those external factors.

REWARD SUCCESS FOR GROUP AND INDIVIDUALS

There is an old joke that the 6 phases of a project are the following:

- Enthusiasm
- Disillusionment
- Panic
- Search for the guilty
- Punishment of the innocent
- Praise and honors for the non-participants

As with most humor, it comes from truth. It is not uncommon to see someone getting an award for their work, while others that contributed get nothing and are left wondering what that other person even did. Too often it seems that the credit goes to those who had the least to do with the effort.

My first job in IT was part of a large project implementing a system. There was a parallel effort at the same time building a new data center. This new system was a key component of that data center.

I was young and had no other obligations. I worked long hours and loved every minute of it. There were times during this project where I would arrive as a shift was ending and people were going home. When they returned to start their next shift 12 hours later, I was still there.

After months of work, we got the project rolled out and despite many challenges, it was a success. The data center was operational, and the new system worked as designed. There was a dedication ceremony for the new data center where leaders gave speeches about the accomplishments.

While names were being called out, there were a lot of names that I did not recognize and some who, from my perspective, only had a cursory involvement. The leaders got through all the accolades, yet something was missing. My name was not mentioned once. I was the lead on this project and devoted a significant portion of my time to making it happen. But it seemed that my contribution was not worthy of a mention. This was terribly disheartening.

The next day I received a memo from the VP over my area. He apologized for overlooking me in his notes. I appreciated the sentiment but couldn't help but feel it was too late. Others were recognized in front of the whole company, I was not. In my mind, all that I had done was less important than whatever the other people had done.

This was an opportunity for leadership to really make people feel good about their work and build some loyalty for the future, but they dropped the ball. Sure, in the grand scheme, it was just an oversight in a speech. I worked there for two more years, and my career has gone just fine in the 20+ years since. But it still hurts a little and it is a lesson that I carry with me.

Do not underestimate the importance of recognition. It does not have to be much, but it needs to be sincere. It will go a long way when people are assessing how they feel about their job and the company as a whole. You, as their leader, have significantly more influence on what someone thinks about the company than anyone else.

Here are a few tips to do recognition right.

Be Specific

Most companies have some sort of program in place where people can recognize others. Through these programs you can send notes thanking them for their work on something. The intention is to encourage people to recognize each other and make sure their leader knows what they've done.

As a manager of many people, I get copied on these communications so that I can see what each person is contributing and provide my own recognition. The disappointing thing is that these notes too often contain only comments such as, "Thanks for your help," or "Nice Job." The person sending it knows what they are thanking the recipient for. And the recipient knows, presumably, what they did to help the sender. But I may not have any idea. There are a lot of tasks that go on in the team each day that a leader simply does not see.

Always make sure when you send recognition, you are very specific. What did the person do that you are thanking them for? What was the outcome that their contribution facilitated? How much of an effort was it for them?

For example, "Thank you so much for your assistance on the Alpha X migration. We were really struggling with the mix ratio optimization and your input helped us turn the corner. I know this took time away from your work on the Beta Y project, but we really appreciate your time."

In 3 sentences, anyone who reads this knows what the person did, how it helped the other team, and the sacrifice they made to provide that assistance. So much better than "Nice job"

Be Sincere

There is a scene in the movie Christmas Vacation, where Clark Griswold is talking to a co-worker when his boss walks by along with his entourage. The boss stops to thank Clark for his work on a new product and asks him to write up a summary of it. Despite repeated attempts, the boss never gets Clark's name right. Later when Clark sees the boss again, the boss has no idea who Clark is and continues to get his name wrong. When Clark asks if the write-up helped, the boss doesn't seem to remember what he is talking about and tries to get on the phone to end the conversation.

This is a textbook case of not being sincere. This boss could not even be bothered to learn the name of the person he was talking to. He clearly never even acknowledged receipt of the write-up he had asked for. From Clark's perspective, this 'leader' did not care about him at all.

You need to make sure your sentiment is clear. You need to know your people. You need to know the sacrifices they make for the company. You need to acknowledge those sacrifices when you recognize them. Don't just walk by and pat them on the shoulder and say "Good job," without even breaking stride. Take a few moments to show them you really value what they did. Show them that you care.

Be on Time

Earlier we talked about how leaders need to be talking to their team regularly. It is not acceptable to go weeks without contact. The worst thing to do is set a goal and then not discuss it until end-of-year reviews. The same is true for all recognition.

If someone did something great on Monday, then sometime no later than Tuesday you should be thanking them for the work. I am not saying everything that someone does requires recognition, but if they did something that warrants a call out, don't wait until Friday to do it. Do it right away. Otherwise, by the time you recognize them, they have already moved on to a dozen other things. The message they get instead is that you don't understand how much they truly do around here.

Whatever format you choose for recognizing people, Be Specific, Be Sincere, Be on Time.

EDUCATION

You've laid out your vision. You've inspired your team. You've been the picture of open communication. The last piece of the puzzle is education. You cannot innovate if you do not keep yourself informed about everything going on around you.

Education takes on many forms. It requires you to reflect on how you achieved your goals. You must learn how to turn setbacks into successes. You need to build on your strengths. And, you must prepare yourself for the future.

Leadership is a cycle. It continually repeats itself. The link that connects each iteration to the next is education. If you do not educate yourself and your team, then you will hit a wall. There is no innovation if you are not actively preparing for it.

SELF-AWARENESS

A line in the Rush song *Freewill* says, "Blame is better to give than receive." It is much easier to point a finger to something else as the cause of a problem than to accept our own failure. But that doesn't make it right and it certainly is not productive.

Leadership is never about being right all the time. In fact, being an innovative leader requires you to be wrong a good percentage of the time. If you are not making mistakes, then it is likely that you are not getting far enough out of your comfort zone.

A leader needs to master the art of reflection, not deflection. You need to be able to look back on your performance as a leader and make adjustments. Every conversation you have with your team, every performance evaluation you give or receive, every memo you write—each is an opportunity to look at how you did and make improvements.

When encountering a setback or receiving negative feedback, a leader does not get defensive and look for a place to shift the blame. A leader acknowledges the situation and takes steps to do better next time.

You might be tempted to look at other leaders and think they have it all together. They always seem to say the right thing and evoke confidence at every turn. In reality, those leaders are likely second-guessing all of their actions. Not because they lack confidence, but because they see every action as an opportunity to learn. This analysis is what allows them to become better leaders.

The least innovative person is the one who thinks they know it all and has the answers to every problem. That is not innovation, that is delusion. How can you innovate if you already think you know everything?

If you are looking for where to start in your journey to be innovative, start with reflection. Look to yourself first. Avoid blaming others. Even in cases where you were not at fault, ask yourself, "But what could I have done that might have helped?"

Leadership is never about knowing the right path. It is about finding the right path. You find it by being self-aware and having the courage to change yourself.

TURN FAILURE INTO SUCCESS

Movies, and most narrative fiction, follows a predictable arc. The story is setup, and the heroes get a challenge of some sort. They seem to overcome the challenge only to be thrown a final, seemingly insurmountable, obstacle just when victory is at hand. They must apply everything they've learned throughout the story to solve this last problem and win the day. Life rarely follows such a defined pattern, but it is entirely likely that you will have situations where it seems you have lost the war.

You have been making progress reducing your delivery times, only to have a critical project encounter an obstacle that can't be overcome, and you miss the deadline. Suddenly everything you did has been thrown into question. People will wonder if your strategy is not sustainable or if it can't scale to large projects. You will be questioned mercilessly, and you will even begin to doubt your abilities as a lead.

Stop that!

There will always be challenges. Some of those challenges will be huge. These are not indicators that your plan is flawed. It is simply an opportunity to learn from new data and build an even better process.

In January of 1967, Gus Grissom, Ed White, and Roger Chafee climbed into the Apollo 1 command module for a test of the systems. The tests did not go well and took longer than expected. While flipping a switch, there was a spark. In the oxygen-rich environment of the command module, a flash fire spread quickly and killed all three men within seconds.

This tragedy in the middle of the space program, and right at the beginning of the phase that was to bring us to the moon, called into question our abilities. What was wrong with the craft? What was wrong with the planning? Why didn't we see this coming?

It is easy to get down when things go awry.

In the case of Apollo 1, three men lost their lives. Rarely do the stakes reach that level.

But it is what you do the next day that matters. You have a choice of packing it in and saying it's just too hard and why are we even trying this. Or you can look at every detail to find out how you can do this better.

Following the Apollo 1 fire, they completely redesigned the command module. Everything from the wiring to the door latches was adjusted to be safer and more resilient. It would be nearly two years before we would launch another man in space. But, within 10 months of returning to space we landed a man on the moon. That success was directly driven by the lessons learned and the renewed determination to achieve the end goal.

You may have a big failure in a project that was missed or an outage that caused impact. But what went right? What did the team do well? What have you learned? If the answers are nothing, nothing, and nothing, then this is truly a failure. But that is likely not the case.

You need to review each step of the process. Play "Monday-morning quarterback." Hindsight is indeed 20/20, so take advantage of that. Look at everything and ask what should have been.

It is especially important that you not assign blame. None of this exercise is about finding guilty parties to blame. It doesn't matter who made the decision. Approach it all as though everyone on the team would have made the same decisions and ask why that is the case. Remember, we are all in this together. If one of us fails, then we all have failed. So, let's work together on the solution.

When you find small successes in there, highlight them as something that went well. If an individual did something well, then it is good to call them out. Remember, as a leader, you take more than your share of the blame, and significantly less than your share of the credit. Your role in this situation is to keep the team motivated. Give them a reason to be optimistic despite the setback.

As you build your new plan, you can highlight all the ways that it is better than what you had. And you can talk about how much you've learned and how that experience will make you better able to adapt to new challenges. There will no doubt be additional setbacks down the road. Nothing is perfect. But, as long as you are committed to learning from the experience then you will be just fine and your team will be better for it.

Setbacks are just that, setbacks. They are not the end of the line. They are opportunities to learn, and grow, and become a better team. If the review is done properly, then the team you have afterwards will be better than the one you had the day before.

BUILD ON STRENGTHS AND SUCCESSES

There is an old axiom in career development that you identify your strengths and weakness and try to use your strengths to improve your weaknesses. If you are great at hitting fastballs, then you need to identify what about hitting a fastball makes them easy for you, and see how you can apply that to hitting curveballs.

It sounds great on paper but can be hard to implement. Often it will seem that the things you do well have little to do with the things you do not excel at. Instead of fastballs vs curveballs, it is fastballs vs grilling steak. So, what can you do?

There are really 2 parts to this.

Apply what you can

If this is a fastball/curveball conversation, then you need to dig into the specifics. What parts of the effort did you do well on? What parts did you not? Imagine, or even physically draw, a Venn diagram showing the detail of each and see where there is overlap.

Your team might be great at the technical stuff, but really struggled with communication. In the communication area, there might be technical communication where you did well. We clearly can communicate, but it is the type of communication that is a hurdle. Okay. Then let's focus on how we can shape messages and adjust conversations to the audience and learn to understand what our clients need. This analysis shows you where you have skills that you can build on and improve.

Offload what you can't

When I go to a restaurant, I am always a little perplexed when I see menus that are 4+ pages long with everything from burgers, to pizza, to seafood, to tacos. Variety is nice, but I must question how often they make some of these items. I mean, if the bulk of the menu is standard fare, such as fried food and spaghetti and sandwiches, but down at the bottom is Duck Pate en Croute, is that really something you want to try? I don't doubt that they COULD make it, but how often do they get an order for it? How out of practice are they? If that is the only Duck Pate dish on the menu, how old is it? Is it frozen?

Use this same analysis for your team. If you are a team built for delivering server projects, but for some reason you are also tasked with managing databases, then you need to question if all the tasks you are doing belong with your team. Perhaps that work should go elsewhere.

Naturally, other teams are not going to just take on more work. You will need to do a thorough analysis and get all the data about how much time this is taking up, and whether you would need to transfer any people to the other team. Maybe it doesn't make sense if it is a small portion of the work, but it is worthy of discussion. Just because something has always been done by your team doesn't mean it should always be done by your team.

Learn from what you do well to fix the things you don't.

SUSTAINABILITY

In one episode of the TV show, The Big Bang Theory, Penny creates these small paper flowers that can be worn in your hair. She calls them Penny Blossoms and sells them online. Eventually, she gets a huge order for them and quickly realizes that she does not have the infrastructure necessary to sustain this growth.

Sustainability means that you can prepare for tomorrow without sacrificing today. Leaders must lead each day while also looking to the future. We must ensure we have the skills to be ready for the next thing that comes along.

How are you going to ensure that your skills will be just as valuable in 10 years as they are today? This comes down to 2 things.

Always be looking for the next thing

Innovative leaders do not wait for something to fail before they try something new. The axiom "If it ain't broke, don't fix it" does not apply. To an innovative leader, if it ain't broke, try harder.

A common sight in the United States is to see people lining up the day before a new release so that they can be among the first to own it. It doesn't matter what it is, they just need to be first. These are the early adopters. They like to be on the cutting edge.

You do not need to be that extreme. It is perfectly fine to allow for trends to develop. The most important thing is to watch for those trends. Where are things going? What is the new technology? What new processes are being developed? How are they doing it at other companies?

Always be asking the questions. When your team is firing on all cylinders, you should already be thinking about what the next disruption will be.

Never believe you have reached the end.

Throughout this book, we've talked about how leadership is a journey, not a destination. There is no end. No matter how much you learn or how much you experience, there is always more. There is always something you can do better.

In the early days of man, the only way to get around was to walk. Eventually, we learned to ride on the backs of animals. Soon we built boats and wagons. Soon we had steam engines to power these vehicles. Then we made trains. Then cars. Then airplanes. Then jets. Now we are on the verge of accessible space transportation. Where does it end?

The answer is, it doesn't.

There is no end. We will develop newer, faster, safer modes of transportation for as long as we exist. Just as the humans building the first wagon could not imagine a spaceship, we cannot hope to visualize what new transportation will be developed two hundred years from now. But, you can be sure it will be developed.

There is nothing wrong with taking a breath when you reach a milestone. It is important to recognize those that contributed to the goal, celebrate the victory, and reflect on what was achieved. Be proud of those accomplishments. Then turn your attention to the future. No matter how substantial, those milestones are never the end.

DO BETTER THINGS

On the TV show *The Wire*, there is a character named Bubbles, played by Andre Royo. Bubbles is a heroin addict who constantly struggles with the desire to get clean and live a normal life. He always encounters obstacles that pull him back to his world of drug abuse.

At one point during his journey, he connects with Waylon, a recovered addict who tries to help others. While Bubbles tries to figure out what to do, Waylon tells him, "Gettin' clean's the easy part. Then comes life."

We tend to look at everything we do as a series of milestones. We are constantly racing to the next destination. We need to complete this project, or we need to get ready for the holidays, or we need to remodel the bathroom. There is always another destination lurking out there for us.

At some point we must enjoy the journey itself.

A few hours from where I live is the Blue Ridge Parkway. This 469-mile road was constructed as part of Franklin Roosevelt's New Deal. It was a way to create jobs. The road is unique in that it has special rules for how it is managed, and it is isolated from other roadways. It is part of the National Park system.

Every other National Park is a destination. You go to see Yellowstone. You go to see Yosemite. You got to see Acadia. But this National Park is about the journey. It has stops along the way, but its purpose is to provide a scenic route for travelers. You can travel any length of its 469 miles and never get anywhere. You just enjoy the view.

You need to find the joy in your team. Once the project is done and the milestones achieved, there is day-to-day work that needs to be done. This work might be passed to another group and maybe your team dissolves, but in most cases, your team now must support this new achievement.

Doing something for the long haul is quite different from a one-time effort. You must deal with issues of scalability, and security, and flexibility more so than at any point during the project.

If what you delivered is truly great, then what you might find is that everyone wants in on it. You completed the project with a few core clients. Now dozens of others want to try it out. Does it scale? Can you support that growth?

Imagine a baker in their kitchen baking cakes for weddings and birthdays. They are starting a business and getting the word out. They handle their first few deliveries and get rave reviews. A few days later word has spread, and they get an order for a dozen cakes. They pull a few all-nighters and meet the commitments. Word spreads some more and they have 3 dozen orders. There is simply no way they can bake all those cakes. They do not have the ovens or the time. They must turn away orders. This hurts their reputation and soon they are struggling to recover. They never planned for the long haul. Up until that moment, it was only about the few destinations. There was no plan for the journey.

There are a few things to consider as you make the transition.

Sustainability

As mentioned above, this is critical. You need to think about how you manage things on a day-to-day basis. Often, projects are completed with the expectation that it will make you more efficient and reduce the need for staff. Do more with less. What usually happens is that the things the staff does is simply different from what they did before. The project really addressed the quality, consistency, and throughput of the work, but still requires the same number of people in different roles. You need to define those roles and redraw the process flows around the new designs. You need something that works for the peaks and valleys that will come. What happens if you get an order tomorrow for three times as many widgets as you have ever delivered? You need to have a plan.

Succession Planning

This is often overlooked, but it is an important part of everyone's career. When thinking about career growth, we become focused on where we are going. We also need to be looking at who will pick up the torch. You did a great job building this team and running this effort. You have been rewarded and you have setup the team for long-term success in the future.

Now what?

When a TV show starts, they will have a team of writers putting out new episodes week after week. They establish the show as a hit and millions of people tune in. The show might run for 10 years, but the writers in year 10 are not the same writers in year 1. Once you achieve success, you move on to greater challenges. Those writers become creators and producers of new shows. You will be offered new projects and asked to start new teams. You can, of course, stay where you are if that is what interests you. But if your desire is to continue moving to different challenges, then you need to plan about who steps in behind you.

Who on your team has the leadership qualities you would expect? Who knows the difference between a supervisor and a manager and a leader? Who can make the transition between being an expert and a leader? And who WANTS to do it? You need to be working on this all though the journey. When you decide to move on, your leader will ask you, "who is in the best position to take your place?" Ideally, you have someone in mind that they can start with. This makes the transition easier and you know that the team will continue generally on the path you put it on.

Self-Care

Building teams is hard. There are a lot of different personalities to manage. There are goals from leadership. There are performance issues and external factors. It can take a toll as you are constantly faced with one challenge after another.

Do not forget to look out for yourself. If you have done your job, then you should be able to step away for a couple weeks and know that the team will continue without you. This is not an indicator that you are not needed, it is a sign that you have done a tremendous job building your team. They are engaged and committed and self-sufficient. That is the goal of any leader. Take advantage of your efforts in building this and step away to recharge your batteries. You will find that, when you return, you are ready to take on greater challenges and lead the team even further.

Just as Edison built upon the work done by those before him, you must always be striving to build your new light bulb. Step out of the comfort zone and into the realm of the unknown. Be prepared to make mistakes and to fail. Those are the moments when true innovation is discovered.

Share your vision. Engage with others. Welcome feedback. Continuously improve. These are the keys that drive all innovation. If you can do these things, then you have positioned yourself to do better things.

ABOUT THE AUTHOR

John Storta Jr has been leading Information Technology projects and teams for Fortune 500 companies for more than 25 years. He enjoys building engaged teams that deliver efficiencies through analytics, innovation, and automation.

His articles and books allow him to share his experiences to help others navigate life.

He lives with his family in North Carolina.

Visit his website, johnstortajr.com, for information on upcoming releases.